Praise for
Where did my son go?

"A heartfelt and personal account of true-life experiences of a father's never-ending commitment and dedication to a son, lost in a world of drug addiction. Through faith and love, Alex preserves to maintain his sanity and values. His resolve to never give up hope is encouragement to any parent who is experiencing this same trauma in their lives."

~Blaine M. Higgs, Former Premier of New Brunswick

"This book is a must read! I highly recommend this book be used as an educational tool in many Recovery Centers far and wide."

~Barb Parker, author of My Sister's Journey from Heartache to Heartache and Don't Leave Me

"We all have times when we feel lost, hurt and asking, 'Where is God in all of this?' In the book, Where did My Son Go?, you will experience the feelings of hopelessness, desperation and disappointment through the very raw and vulnerable writing of the journey parenting a child imprisoned by addiction and mental health [disorders]. It's a riveting story that will leave you breathless and in awe of the amazing grace that comes from none other than Jesus Himself."

~Sandra Norton, wife, mother of three, grandmother to five beautiful granddaughters, and author of Finding Me, published through Joppa House Publishing.

"Alex's story is one of cherished memories, pain, loss and grief. He gives us a real and honest look at the heart of a father who must struggle to balance his deep love and heartbreak for his son. He is also brutally honest about the

battles, lessons and black holes along the path of dealing with the aftermath of addiction.

"Through it all he learns to trust and lean on a Jesus who knows the full story and who cares for him deeply. This is a must-read for anyone who is trying to figure out how to walk next to someone who is lost to their bad choices!"

-Kevin and Laura Myers. Kevin is senior pastor at Brazil Lake Wesleyan Church in Nova Scotia

WHERE DID MY SON GO?

A FATHER'S REFLECTIONS ON DRUG ABUSE, LOSS AND FIGHTING TO KEEP FAITH

ALEX DAGGETT

Copyright © 2025 Alex Daggett
All poems are original work published with author's permission Copyright © 2025 Joanne Daggett

Scriptures taken from the Holy Bible, New International Version®, NIV®. Copyright © 1973, 1978, 1984, 2011 by Biblica, Inc.™ Used by permission of Zondervan. All rights reserved worldwide. www.zondervan.com The "NIV" and "New International Version" are trademarks registered in the United States Patent and Trademark Office by Biblica, Inc.™
ISBN: 979-8-9872117-5-5

Cover Illustration, Layout, and Interior:
Anna Rhea | joppahousepublishing.com

First printing edition 2025 in the United States of America and Canada

This paper meets the requirements of ANSI/NISO Z39.48-1992 (Permanence of Paper).

Published by Joppa House Publishing
Dallas, Tx

https://joppahousepublishing.com/

Dedication

To Joanne

For keeping the faith,
holding my hand, never giving up,
and making me laugh along the journey.

All my love.

Table of Contents

Foreword

Few words in the English language carry as much weight as "Father" and "Son." Perhaps it's because we all have fathers, or because so many of us are sons, or have sons of our own. These words are more than just titles—they hold stories, histories, and emotions that run deep. Few things in life have the power to shape us, break us, heal us, and define us quite like our fathers or the experience of becoming one. Fatherhood is a calling unlike any other, a sacred responsibility that brings both unspeakable joy and an undeniable weight. It reveals both the best and the broken within us, illuminating what is right in the world while exposing what is not. There is something profoundly transcendent about fatherhood, a divine imprint woven into our very being that points us toward what should be—while at the same time confronting us with the reality of what is. It is one of life's greatest blessings, yet also one of its heaviest burdens. It is, in every sense, a beautiful struggle.

In Where Did My Son Go?, *we see this paradox of pain and beauty unfold in striking detail. Alex Daggett offers a deeply personal and profoundly moving account of love, loss, faith, and resilience, inviting us into the raw and complex reality of fatherhood. Through his own journey—one that has seen both the boundless joys of parenthood and great depths of sorrow—Alex tells a story that is at times heartbreaking and yet, truly hopeful.*

In a world where so many suffer in silence, weighed down by struggles they feel they must carry alone, Alex's story shines as a beacon of hope and healing. With honesty and vulnerability, he walks us through his own pain, his questions, and his unwavering faith in a God who remains present in every season—especially in the hardest ones. His journey is not just one of survival, but of transformation, offering encouragement to anyone who has ever wrestled with grief, faith, or the complexities of parenthood.

Whether you are a parent who knows this struggle firsthand, a friend or family member supporting a loved one, or simply a reader searching for a story of resilience, hope, and the never-ending love of God, you will find something deeply moving in these pages. Alex Daggett has given us a book that is raw, poetic, and profoundly human—a story that will linger in your heart long after you turn the final page.

Pastor. Father. Son.

~Brent Ingersoll, Senior Pastor, King's Church, Quispamsis

Chapter 1
My Dad

"The heart of a father is the masterpiece of nature."

—Antoine François Prévost

"We all have a father. But few have a dad. I was blessed with the best of both."

—Alex Daggett

He's failing fast.

My brother's message confirmed the heartbreaking reality. He had been texting me every few minutes about our father's condition. There was only a small pause before the final text.

He's gone Al. It was very fast and very peaceful.

And just like that, Dad passed. It was a punch to my stomach, but worse, it was a breaking of my soul.

The family knew it was coming. In September of 2022 at the age of eighty-five, my father, Claude, had been diagnosed with terminal cancer. There would be no experimental treatments, no rounds of chemo. Instead he opted to spend his last months with us taking medications that kept him alive through Thanksgiving and Christmas. I firmly believe he put on a good front, but through the smiles, I know the cancer was digging its claws into him. He must have felt terrible. Through the winter of 2023 his health declined rapidly. Within that time, he had a stroke, a vicious repercussion of his illness. Three weeks later on Good Friday, he passed away.

Dad was the best of the best. Through his last few months between the four of us children, there must have been a hundred calls and texts. We traveled back and forth to the island to be there for Mom. That Friday night, I was home in Quispamsis, about three hours away, and was planning to go see Dad the next morning. My sisters, Crystal and Amy (both of whom live in our hometown of Grand Manan), and my brother, Andy (who lives six hours east on Prince Edward Island), had arrived to see our dad that evening at the hospital. I'm grateful my siblings and my mom were able to see my dad off to his eternal home. It hurt to miss being in his presence during his final moments, but when I returned home a few days earlier there was nothing left unsaid. I knew how much my dad loved us. In the last three weeks, the stroke has taken his ability to speak, but we agreed that Dad had shown his love by example, so we didn't need any more words from him to confirm our and his feelings. He knew, we all knew. He was a pillar both in our family and community.

Dad passed one month shy of his eighty-sixth birthday that following May. What an extraordinary life he had lived. Our parents had just celebrated their sixty-fifth wedding anniversary the previous November. Their marriage is a testament of true love and whole-hearted commitment that seems to be so rare these days. There are so many memories of their journey together that it could take up the pages of a novel in order to share them. Even then, I would need the right words to express the depth of their devotion.

I attribute their lasting union to their faith. We were brought up in a Christian home. However, I am truly blessed that it wasn't just "Christian" on Sundays, at meetings, or out in public. Their commitment to God was never just a title to wear. Both Mom and Dad lived out their faith with the purist love and most genuine sincerity.

A big man at six-foot-three in his prime, I looked up to my dad as a man who loved his wife and family, but he was even greater than that. He was a man of service, accepting a position as a member of his church's deacons board as well as the Rotary Club and was a school board chairman for a number of years. German priest, Martin Luther, once said, "Good works do not make a good man, but a good man does good works."[1] Yes, Dad loved sports, his work, the Red Sox, fishing, teaching Sunday School, golf, and Florida in the winter months. He cherished time with friends. But, in the end, his priorities were always God and family.

At the funeral service, my brother and I delivered the

---

[1] Luther, M. (1903). *Christian Liberty* (p. 56). Lutheran Publication Society.

eulogy. While at the platform facing the attendants, we were amazed at how many people had come to pay their respects. Many of dad's friends had died before him, but there were people of all ages at the service. Our family was encouraged to see how many people dad had inspired as he led his life by example. On this small island, he had affected so many lives in encouraging ways. His loss brought so many others together to grieve for a man whose legacy could be seen in each teary eye.

Mom had asked Andy and I to keep it light and add some humor to our eulogy as we told stories of Dad. When we were first discussing what to say and what stories to tell, we each came up with ten to twelve stories but realized we needed to cut it back to four or five stories each. We could have talked for hours. We just had so many cherished memories of growing up with our dad.

One of my favorites can give you a glimpse of what he was like. When I was about fourteen, my brother and a few friends would spend the night in an old camper in our backyard. One night, I stayed alone, planning to meet some friends after midnight down at the "crick," the nickname for a part of our town where a creek flowed through under a concrete bridge. This crick flowed into the world's largest tides in the Bay of Fundy. Many of my younger years were spent swimming, fishing, canoeing, and hanging out by that bridge in the crick. I stepped out of the camper and started across the back yard. It was a beautiful, quiet, clear August night with the moon and stars illuminating the sky. It would be perfect for staying out all night! Smiling at the thought of our overnight adventure, I walked on. However, I was halfway through the yard when I heard a loud, booming voice.

"Alex! Where do you think you are going?"

For a split second, I wondered if the ominous voice I heard was Claude or God?

Halting in my tracks, it took only another second to know it was Dad. No need to answer. I turned immediately as he ordered me into the house. I was given a choice to stay in the house or in the camper, but there would be no roaming around town with my pals that night. I believe that fall evening was spent in the comfort of my own bed.

Dad had the quickest wit and best humor when it came to involving his four children. My sisters, who are seven and five years older than I, loved to tease and pick on my brother and me. Usually it was all in fun, but other times it would get a bit out of hand and inevitably someone got angry. One evening, I was in my bedroom and Amy was in hers. Suddenly, I heard screaming and crying, and my mom hollered for my dad to go help stop the ruckus. I ran to the source of the commotion to find Andy sitting on Crystal, pinning her to the floor. He was on her back and had one of her arms up behind her and her head held to the floor. Crystal was screaming for Andy to stop, but at that point he was mad because of whatever she had done to him and he wasn't giving in to her cries.

Within a few seconds Dad was on the scene and shouted, "Stop!"

We froze.

He calmly looked at my mom and said, "Helen, I've been telling the girls for the last couple of years that the boys are getting stronger and that their day would come. Well, it just showed up."

With that, he split them up and after that day no one messed with Andy again. In fact, I still don't because his broad shoulders and thick arms made me think twice before tackling him, even for fun.

That was my dad. He understood being a teenager and having siblings. He used humor to deal with tricky situations. But he also knew when to lay down the law, so to speak, when one of us went too far. I cherish these memories and so many more like them.

You may wonder why I am telling you first about my dad when the book is intended to be about my son. You may wonder where my dad's story applies to the bigger context of this book. You see, I thought everyone had a dad like mine. Not until I reached my teenage years did I realize that not all kids were as blessed or as fortunate. Not all wives or in-laws had a man like this in their lives who brought love and laughter into each day. There is no man that I looked up to and respected more than my dad. He had such a balanced approach and outlook on faith, work, love, and life, and I only wish I could be half as good as he was. Mostly, it was his wisdom that I really appreciated and now miss every single day. I wish I could call him one more time for a word of advice and to say, "Keep me and my family in your prayers, Dad."

Being a dad isn't easy, and these days it's even more difficult than ever in this fast-paced world. Thoughts and reflections of my dad take me quickly to my son and flood my mind with so many memories, both good and bad.

"Fathers encourage and comfort their children."

—1 Thessalonians 2:11-12

Chapter 2

My Son

"What gives me the most hope every day is God's grace."

—Rick Warren

"Anything can happen to anyone at any time."

—Alex Daggett

I think every man has plans for the future. Many of those dreams include a wife and family, maybe a couple of children. Mine included a son to teach how to play hockey, ride a bike, throw and catch a ball, fish, hunt, and drive his first car. These dreams became plans when my time came to be a father. I taught both of my daughters most of those things. But my son...that is where this story really starts.

Greg came into my life in the most unique, yet tragic way. I met my wife, Joanne, at school as we grew up in the same village of Seal Cove on Grand Manan Island. After graduation, I went off to university, and we went our separate ways like many high school sweethearts. Joanne graduated the following year and married someone else. Life took us in different directions as it often does. Soon, Joanne was pregnant. On a few occasions, our paths crossed with a smile, a friendly hello, but nothing more. I went on to community college to pursue my carpentry training in the fall of 1986.

Shortly after I started school, I received a phone call. Joanne had given birth to a son. This should have been joyous news for her family, but there was more to her story than I could have imagined. Her husband, Arthur, had died in a car accident on his way to the hospital to see his wife and new baby boy. Hearing this, I was struck with a flood of emotions that overwhelmed me that night and for the following days. How was she doing? How could she, at almost nineteen years old, become a mom and a widow on the same day? I couldn't even begin to imagine the depth of her pain.[1]

I spent the fall semester consumed by thoughts and feelings for her. I wondered how she could possibly cope with such an enormous tragedy and have to wake up every day to care for her precious baby. During that time, I was in a serious relationship with another girl when all of this

[1] Joanne shares her personal story and path with God in her book, *Sing Dance Pray: A Collection of Prose and Poetry Through Life's Journey.*

happened. By that Christmas, my heart was all over the place.

I decided to visit Joanne and her son, Greg, during the holiday break while I was home on Grand Manan Island for a few weeks. We talked on a regular basis by phone, and through those conversations, I knew where my heart and mind were pulling me. I couldn't lie to myself nor to my girlfriend. I broke off our relationship and gave myself fully to Joanne. Our dates were filled with hours-long talks about life, the complicated paths ahead, her situation with a newborn son and all that involved. Because of our connection in high school and growing up in the same village, we already had a strong foundation of trust. It was easier and even more natural to make plans for our future with Greg as our central focus.

We were married in August of 1987 and began attending my hometown church, Seal Cove Baptist. We grew our family by two daughters (both beautiful inside and out) who would complete our family. I built our home in 1992. It was a place filled with fun, love, Sunday chicken after church, many family parties, and kids all the time because our children had many friends. Our family was involved in different church and school activities. Though busy, life seemed simpler and easier, as days turned into weeks then melted into years. The kids grew up, and Joanne and I walked through life together. We were a family unit. We were blessed more than we knew, and although busy, we wouldn't have wanted it any other way.

Greg was our first child though, in the beginning, he wasn't legally mine. A year after we were married, my grandfather, a retired lawyer, was tasked with writing up Greg's adoption papers so that he could take my family name. Grampy K was happy to do this for us. By the fall of 1988, the adoption went through. I can still remember that feeling of joy and pride when Greg, who had been mine in my heart, finally had my last name.

Sometimes it seems like he came into my life just the other day. At times it seems like so very long ago. I felt so strongly that I was given this boy to raise, to be part of my life, that God had brought us all together for a reason. Don't get me wrong...I still feel like this at times, but it's different and so much harder now as I will explain in the next few chapters.

A good friend of mine, a great man and dad who has faced unbelievable heartache, once told me, "Alex, there's not much in this life that can bring you more joy or more pain than your children." I will never forget that and how it impacted me. Sadly, he sure was right. I learned this more and more as we walked down the road of life as a family. Yet, I never imagined the incredible depth of heartbreak we would endure.

To tell this story from the perspective of a husband and father, I have to also tell my family's story and our son's precarious journey. As much as I share, there are so many more details that are too personal and too painful to express. Primarily, I don't want to demean or hurt my son in any way despite all the hurt, trauma, grief, and heartache that he has caused our family. Much of that is his story to share, and how much he chooses to disclose in the future is up to him. I pray daily that someday God will use him and his story to help others as well as himself. However, in order for my thoughts to make sense, some discrete elements of his story need to be told.

"His father saw him and was filled with compassion for him."

—*Luke 15:20*

Joanne holding Greg on our wedding day.

Chapter 3

"D" Requirements

"However low you are, there is always something to be proud of, and however high you are, there is always something to humble you."

—Megyn Kelly

"Some days just seem routine then one phone call can change it all."

—Alex Daggett

Greg was a lot of fun back when he was younger. Everyone loved his sense of humor, quick wit, and skateboarding tricks. He was goodhearted. His concern for others, and his musical talents were a blessing to many. As I stated earlier, life was good in so many ways as we lived life with our children and lots of family and friends.

In July of 2002, my wife and I made the decision to sell our house and move from Grand Manan Island to the town of Quispamsis, New Brunswick. Greg was starting grade eleven that fall, our eldest daughter, Marissa, was entering grade nine, and our youngest, Holly, into grade five. Transitioning from a high school of nearly two hundred students to a much larger school of approximately twelve hundred was a huge adjustment for Greg and Marissa.

Looking back now, though, I think overall the move was harder for Marissa, especially at her age as she didn't have as many connections to the other students like her brother did. Greg seemed to fit in quickly and easily because he already knew a few teens from church and from camps he had worked at and rallies he had attended. Still, it was a big adjustment to a new culture with so many more students. But, he rose to be a top-notch student, participating in student council and making many new friends in those last two years of high school. He even found a home in theater, acting and singing in the awesome musicals the school put on annually. How we loved going to those!

Greg had a talent for music. He could sing any harmony and play guitar and piano. The musicals gave him a chance to show off his dancing skills. I think he drew his joy from entertaining. How could he not? His upbeat personality attracted others to him. His keen mind extended beyond academics, a God-given gift that I encouraged him to use in whatever way he felt called. Most teens will test the waters with their parents and do things that they know they shouldn't. Not so much with Greg. He really didn't push any boundaries or rebel through his teen years. He was great to have around the house hanging out with his friends. I don't say these things to brag, but later you will understand why it crushed my soul to see him lose and walk away from all his potential and talents.

Following graduation, he was chosen by the local Rotary club to represent our area as an exchange student, traveling to Brazil for a ten-month period. We thought this was an exciting opportunity for him. Joanne and I agreed to house an exchange student in return. This would mark the start of a downward spiral that would eventually leave our son spinning out of control. It would lead to devastating experiences that we never saw coming nor even imagined.

In the fall of 2004, we drove Greg to the airport and through hugs and tears, we said good-bye, wishing him all the best in this amazing opportunity. Months flew by. In the spring of 2005, I received a phone call from a representative of Rotary International who informed us that our son would be coming home early. The phone call was short and to the point: Greg had been caught using drugs.

Rotary International had a list of "D" requirements an exchange student must follow: no dating, driving, drinking or drugs. With a zero tolerance for drugs, Greg's Brazilian experience ended. The news kicked me hard in the stomach which left me breathless as I climbed the stairs to share the news with Joanne. I will never forget that crushing phone call, what house we were living at the time, where I was headed that morning, and how it would be the start of what would rock our lives for years to come.

"Do not be anxious about anything, but in every situation, by prayer and petition, with thanksgiving, present your requests to God."

—Philippians 4:6

Chapter 4
My Son Returns Home

"Christians are not perfect, by any means, but they can be made people fully alive."

—Philip Yancey

"People today seem lost, lonely and longing for something, but just don't know what it is."

—Alex Daggett

On Easter weekend 2005, Greg returned home. The days in between the phone call and his return left us overwhelmed with many questions and unknowns. My wife's parents were visiting with us for Easter, and they had no idea why Greg was home so soon, so we decided not to discuss much until the following week. At the same time, we were still hosting an exchange student from Belgium who had become part of our family, staying with us for the first and last term of his visit to New Brunswick. We still talk and think about him with fondness and try to stay in contact with him now that he has grown into an adult, and is married with children. Needless to say, that spring we had a full house.

Between Easter weekend and when our exchange student would head home, we endured a trying and strange time. Greg returned a very different person and barely talked to us which was painful and confusing. We learned about some things that happened in Brazil, but others we may never know and to be honest I'm not sure we ever would *want* to know.

Summer arrived and Greg went back to the camp he had worked at and we thought (as he led us to believe) that things were somehow better by then. We needed to believe that everything was okay.

However, that fall was devastating as Joanne and I realized that our son had been lying to us, still using drugs, and making us believe time and time again that he was better. We attended courses, reached out to friends for advice, and read books to try to learn how to handle a situation we were completely unprepared for. But it only got worse. Greg's uncle agreed to allow Greg to visit and to see if this different environment could help in some way. Greg stayed with him and his family from the fall until the spring of 2006. Joanne and I spoke to him a number of times through those months and hoped and prayed that he was doing better. We agreed for him to return home since he appeared to be improving and walking on a new path. His uncle wasn't completely convinced of this, but we had hoped these months of separation would give him a new perspective.

Greg returned home and in the fall left for university to work on a four year degree. He left for university for four years. It was good for him, but at times he was very down and seemed "off," which could possibly have been depression or potentially another undiagnosed mental illness. We, of course, supported him and would help talk him through it all. Maybe if these issues had derailed him from his path earlier, an intervention could have taken place. But it didn't. Despite the emotional trouble, he went on to graduate from Kingswood University in the spring of 2010 with plans to head to Acadia Divinity College the following fall semester. On the surface, it seemed like he overcame those previous obstacles, matured, and became responsible for his own actions. We were thrilled that he was committed to this plan and that he was in a relationship.

Looking back now we wonder if Greg truly was better. We asked ourselves if he was indeed still using drugs? Was he dealing with too much stress from school? There are so many unanswered questions from that time that still haunt us. In hindsight, we may always be left hanging in the balance between hope and doubt. When was that turning point and was there ever anything in our power that could have changed the outcome?

Greg and his girlfriend married on December 31, 2010. He returned to Acadia in January while she was completing her degree at another university. By the fall, they moved to Nova Scotia in order for Greg to continue the second year of his Master of Arts in Theology at Acadia. They were soon pregnant, and our first granddaughter was born in the spring of 2012. After graduation, they moved back to New Brunswick and lived with us for a few months until they found their own place, and Greg had secured a job. A second child, a son, was born in the spring of 2014.

During this time period from 2012 to 2016, so many things in our son's life became out of control. This is where many personal details must remain buried as they are so deeply devastating and chaotic that it left us reeling and even fractured as a family. What happened during this dark time shocked and nearly destroyed us as Greg chose a dark path. He and his wife would separate, get back together months later, only to finally separate again for good. Unbelievably, our son had become someone we didn't know, couldn't help, and who was completely out of control. Addiction, mental illness, incarceration, and homelessness became realities in Greg's life after his separation in 2016.

From 2016 through 2021, I fought my own health battles. I suffered with depression in the midst of my heartache and questioned God as our family stumbled over a rocky road that we had never dreamed possible. We honestly didn't know how to navigate. I would learn how grief could take over the spirit and turn it to anger. An anger like I'd never dealt with before.

Even now it hurts to write these words while reflecting on those agonizing years. Words will never adequately describe the level of pain and crisis we went through. If not for my friends, my wife (who was in agony herself), my parents, and the prayers of many caring people I probably would not have made it. A couple we knew, who had experienced a similar situation as us, offered us invaluable advice. I still remember this friend looking straight at me and saying, "Alex, be careful. You've got to deal with this soon, or you won't believe where it can take you." He was talking of my grief twisting into anger, and I now realize exactly how true his wise words were. Later on, in this journey, I would have to deal with this grief/anger issue in my life as it inevitably completely consumed me.

"As for me and my household, we will serve the Lord."

—Joshua 24:15

Chapter 5

Grief and Anger

"I sat with my anger long enough until she told me her real name was grief."

—C.S. Lewis, *A Grief Observed*

"Just when you think you have control of grief and anger it sneaks up on you again."

—Alex Daggett

Grief is like the double-edged sword Hebrews 4:12 mentions in that "[i]t cuts all the way into us, where the soul and the spirit are joined. And it judges the thoughts and feelings in our hearts...." When we experience loss, we need to grieve and take the time to process it. Grief hits like a ton of bricks and often when we are not expecting it. At night, it crawls in bed with you. On dark cloudy days, it looms over you. At times it's short, and other times you can't shake it for days. My wife's poem, "The Intruder," captures this sentiment so well.

⚜
The Intruder

Grief - you showed up like the mean bully intruder
you are.

Rude.

You barge in and tear my heart to shreds.

You hurl insults, bring up memories that were locked
away

and taunt me with my unfulfilled heart-longings.

You flash searingly painful reminders of things I've
lost.

That's what you're like, and why I try to avoid you.

Lock the door and close the window shades to keep
you locked out.

I don't want you here.

You're not invited or wanted.

I don't know why you came, exactly, but I knew you
would.

It was inevitable.

Even after all the trying, learning, coping, walking
forward

doing all the things to keep you at bay

you brazenly waltz in and take a seat at my table.

You slither under the pretty tree lit with soft lights

and hung with keepsake ornaments.

Into my peaceful abode you charge

with bold loud ungraceful footsteps.

I don't want you here — no.

If I could punch you in the face, I would!

But I knew you would arrive.

Does it make you happy when my heart rips open,

and tears fall unchecked down my cheeks?

When I want to lay my head back down on a soft pillow and dream

until well past Christmas?

I'm not sure how to keep walking through December with you.

I try to remember what I know to be true and I cling to those truths for dear life.

Then I rest my head on His shoulder.

The ever-present, faithful and kind Abba.

Daddy.

He knows all this hard — and He feels all the grief.

He isn't scared by my pain and grief.

He patiently, tenderly takes my hand in His strong fatherly one.

He holds me gently and whispers

"Cry if you need to."

And I do.

I do.

The one thing I do know for sure, in it all and through it all

— the ugly grief and pain — is that I'm not alone.

Not abandoned.

Never alone.

My faithful Father — the most Beautiful One — He walks with me.

Immanuel — here with me.

He leads me and sometimes carries me.

Amen.—

⚜

From 2012 to 2020, I experienced a huge amount of grief for varying reasons that stemmed from what I had happening in my life. My son's out-of-control behavior was the most significant reason. Other contributing factors included a career change, ongoing health conditions that I struggled with since 2003, providing a home and support for our daughter-in-law and our grandchildren, and my wife's ongoing heartbreak. In the midst of this, our youngest daughter, who had separated from her then husband, needed us and our oldest and her family moved out west, far from us.

This compounded my grief until it was transformed into anger. I was angry at my son for his choices and at how it affected our family so much. I was angry at the church as I didn't feel they were reaching out to help Greg. I was angry at life for not turning out the way I had planned. And honestly, I was angry at God who knew, even when I didn't, that whole time that this destructive emotion stemmed from my hurt and suffering." Grief is like the ocean. It comes in waves, ebbing and flowing. Sometimes the water is calm, and sometimes it is overwhelming. All we can do is learn to swim".-Vicki Harrison

My wife and I began seeing a Christian counselor, and we still do when needed. Bless her soul, our counselor has helped us so much that I don't know what we would have done without her. It was at one of our sessions that she brought my bubbling anger to light without me even realizing it. I broke down. I shared with her that I had reached a point where I was almost ready to explode. She explained that it was my constant grief that was controlling my other emotions, eventually developing into anger. For years I did what I could so as not to take it out on anyone. I tried to keep it from work and my wife. I couldn't let it hinder my relationship with my daughters or grandchildren. But it was always there, just beneath the surface, ready to rear its ugly head whenever we got more bad news concerning Greg.

There are many clichés about the depth of a parent's love. Everyone has a favorite, just scroll through your social media of choice and you will come across many memes. But there are some that we parents fear, those about loss and death. One of which is "There is no greater pain in life than for a parent to lose a child." Well, I had not buried my son, but I had completely lost him. He was lost in so many ways, and I was left wondering if he would ever come back to the kind-hearted, joyful light I remembered. He was lost and had lost. He lost his family, friends, and jobs, and burned so many bridges with nearly everyone. I was left grieving over all of this, day after day, week after week, as months turned into years.

I told our counselor, "These past few years have been a roller coaster ride of never-ending grief."

Her response: "You are actually facing a never-ending but ever-changing grief."

Wow! I will never forget the truth of her words. I still think about them from time to time.

As you watch someone you deeply love spiral out of control and there's nothing you can do to help them, it's a devastating and helpless feeling. As a husband and father, I just want to fix the situation. Many times, I thought I *was* when, in fact, I had no effect at all. As a Christian, I knew the Bible verses that promised that life wouldn't be easy and would in fact bring many trials and troubles. At times while I was embedded with my torn emotions, those verses would make me angry again. It felt like I was carrying too many heavy burdens and that my prayers weren't being answered (at least the way I wanted them to). I was unable to cope, to bear the weight of so much grief and anger.

Benjamin Franklin says, "In life we can be assured of two things, death and taxes." I believe his words should be altered to include a harsher truth: "In life we can be assured of three things, death, taxes, *and loss.*" Regardless of the path we walk in life we will all face loss at some point and grief accompanies most loss. Mine is a "never-ending, ever-changing" grief that I wake to each morning. Even now.

"The Lord is near to the brokenhearted and saves the crushed in spirit."

—Psalms 34:18

Chapter 6

Father's Day

"The influence of a father can either build or destroy, and our world needs more of the former. We have more than enough of the latter. My challenge to you this Father's Day is to add value to someone else."

—John Maxwell

"For many people holidays, special occasions, and hallmark moments are both joyful and sad. That is Father's Day for me, much to be happy and thankful for but also many mixed emotions."

—Alex Daggett

Sunday, June 16, 2024. It is Father's Day. A day that I used to get excited about and fully enjoy. Don't get me wrong, I still do enjoy it and have many blessings to be thankful for. Yet, it now feels very different for me. My own father is gone, and this year feels harder than the last. Last year, our family was in deep mourning because my loving father had recently died the previous April, but the reality of his death hadn't quite sunk in as much. It felt more like he was away on a trip for the weekend. Or that he was only away from the phones so that I couldn't simply call to say hello. This year, though, his death stings a bit more. I don't have to buy him a card. I don't have to call to tell him how much I love and appreciate him although I want to more now than ever. Even writing these words makes the void grow larger somehow. But my siblings and I were fortunate because we knew we had a loving and kind father who was a man of God and who provided a safe home for his family. I have so many great memories that I will treasure forever.

Thanks, Dad.

Today also is a day of mixed feelings and emotions.

Will my son even remember it's Father's Day?

Will he think of his own children?

Will he call me today?

Now that his family is fractured, he no longer sees his kids, so does he want *me* to wish *him* a happy Father's Day?

Our son lost custody of his children and, by this point, has not seen them in six years. This reality causes me a lot of distress, and I am riddled with unanswered questions almost daily. The accompanying grief is gut-wrenching to say the very least.

Joanne and I remain in close contact with our daughter-in-law and her children over the past several, chaotic years. We have hosted them overnight, held

40

birthday parties, shared holiday weekends, and family events. We supported her, helping to lighten her load in any way we could. Though their presence is filled with love and joy, there is always a lingering shadow. Greg isn't with us during those times. He doesn't sit at our happy, festive table and hasn't for many years. We grieve his absence over and over again. The pain does not seem to lessen but only grows when we see that empty chair that marks another moment without him.

When I think of my parents and all that *family* has meant to them, and us, it is so hard to imagine the reality of these circumstances. It's unthinkable, honestly. The hopes and dreams we had for our only son and promise of a wonderful life with the family he created are now shattered.

So, for me, Father's Day is a wonderful day to celebrate with my wife, our daughters and our grandchildren. But it continues to be a very heavy, sad day as I wish my son was here seated with us at our table again. I don't think the aching loss and the hundred questions and unanswered prayers will ever go away. Daily surrender, turning my all over to God again and again. *Why is my family in this place?* I may never know. I do know that I must *choose joy through faith* each day, even in the midst of the pain, hurt, struggle, and crisis. It's not easy, but necessary.

"The Lord is close to the brokenhearted and saves those who are crushed in the spirit."

—Psalm 34:18

Chapter 7

My Wife

"If I had just one wish, my lovely wife, I would choose to spend the rest of my days with you."

—Unknown

"I have been blessed in so many ways but the greatest of all is my beautiful godly wife."

—Alex Daggett

This year, 2025, my wife and I will celebrate our 38th wedding anniversary. Each passing year I realize how fast the previous years have flown by. I remember being in my early twenties, a newly married young father, and hearing the older people say, "The older you get the faster time goes by." I'm sure I didn't believe it and couldn't grasp the truth of it, but I sure do now! Now that I have adult children in their thirties and seven grandchildren, the reality of that saying is crystal clear.

What can I say to describe my wife after we have walked these many years together? There is no one I know who has a deeper faith than she does, who loves Jesus so much, and has a genuine trust in the goodness and grace of God. I have witnessed her endure her own pain and grief as she came to realize that the future she had prayed for, uplifting her son to have the life God deemed for Greg, had been destroyed.

Joanne wasn't even 20 years old when she became a mother and widow on the same rainy September day. She faced indescribable joy and unimaginable grief. Yet, during that tragic time, she felt God draw very near to her and give her inexplicable peace. Though she had every right, she didn't become bitter or turn against God.

Beautifully, and by God's kindness, our lives intertwined on an August afternoon, and we became a unit, which grew to a family of five, with love at the center of it all. Years later, her steadfast strength was tested again and again as the son she had been given, and who she loved so deeply, became a broken man. A man who, in her words, "became lost in a world he couldn't find." It tore me apart inside watching her clinging to God as she struggled in the turmoil of having no ability to save him. Her hurt mirrored mine, even as I tried to hide how it impacted me. We both struggled to make sense of how our son's life fell to ruin by his own hand. What could we do? What could we have done?

Joanne and I were blessed to have been raised by loving, godly parents. We each had great childhood memories. So in the midst of the mess, we wondered about and wrestled with questions like, What did we miss? What went wrong? How did we get here? Why was our son acting in such a destructive way? And how do we cope daily as a family? We struggled to find answers to most of the questions as we watched our family fracturing and tossing about on the waves of uncertainty, chaos, crisis, and fear. Tears fell and prayers breathed as we toiled through these years.

Joanne kept her faith (more than I) and rebuked the negative thoughts and voices attacking her. I have seen my wife down, hurt, and struggling at times over the years, but the heartache our son was putting us through was a totally different and much deeper level of anguish. Years of our son's drug abuse, mental illness, homelessness, and incarceration took a toll on her like I had never seen before, and as her husband I so badly wanted to make it all better for her.

After years of carrying this burden and trying every way she knew how to emotionally endure the weight of it, she turned to a counselor for help (the same one I mentioned in Chapter 5), and soon I joined her. We sat across from the counselor once a month for many years and poured out our hearts. After some time, she asked Joanne to start journaling to help process some of the grief. At first, she didn't want to. Joanne is a reader and didn't see herself as a writer. She didn't think she could fully express her emotions in words. However, our counselor and I encouraged her over the course of a few months until she finally agreed.

Joanne hesitantly started writing down the words of encouragement that she would hear from God. As she walked and listened, His words came to her in the form of poems, stories, prayers of lament and even hope. As she wrote her story, she soon realized that she was writing His story, too. One that told of hope, peace, and joy found in Him, even in the midst of the trials and tribulations. It was inspiring for me to watch this unfold and to read her inspired words. Through the process of writing, a time of healing began for us both.

A year later a book came together from her writings, called Sing Dance Pray. Even though she never seriously considered the idea of writing a book, the support of family, friends, and others who loved her poems, prayers, and prose gave her the confidence to believe it could become a reality. God opened every door leading her to the day her published book was placed in her hands. Her book was healing for me as well. It encouraged others as they read about her faith and hope in God, and as she vulnerably shared her journey of grief but also of hope in her kind Shepherd, her Heavenly Father.

I tell you all this because I believe it was a turning point in our healing. It is also a testament to her saying "yes" to God, doing what she felt God was asking of her. Through her writings, she has kept me moving forward, even when I didn't want to, and encouraged my heart to keep on having faith even in the face of doubt and discouragement. She may be petite, just a tiny girl from a tiny fishing village, but she has a beautiful big heart with such a strong faith and understanding of God. I never take for granted that we still hold hands, still love taking walks together, still love one another deeply, and enjoy each other's company. When I see her across the room, she is still the one my heart yearns to be with.

I don't know which is more difficult—going through a trial yourself or watching someone you love struggling through one. I knew how much she was hurting inside yet she was still doing all she could do to support and encourage me and our daughters, while also navigating day-to-day life. I continued to deal with my own grief, anger, and discouragement, but watching her struggle broke my heart. We were both trying to keep our heads above water, so to speak. I wanted to take away her pain and help her believe that somehow everything would be okay.

I wanted to fix the unfixable while knowing that I couldn't.

To this day, Joanne still has a piece of her heart missing, and it is no small sliver, as so much has changed for our son and his family. Our grandkids are still a huge part of our lives, but circumstances have changed so that we see them less often now than we did in the past. But we know we are blessed in so many ways despite the changes life has brought.

Now that my daughters are grown and are wives and mothers, I see many of Joanne's qualities and personality traits in them. I am so thankful for both and appreciate how they encouraged me and lifted my spirits, even on my darkest days. They both love God, their husbands, and children and shine with beauty from within and without. If beauty is skin deep, as they say, then they have very thick skin! My words are barely adequate enough to express how much they mean to me. The beautiful love notes they write inside my Father's Day or birthday cards bring me so much joy. They too have struggled with losing their brother and have had to process their own pain and grief.

Sadly, every family member must deal with the path of devastation left by an addict's choices. I am thankful that my wife and daughters have chosen to walk a path of better, not bitter. Only God can help me in my daily walk of turning to Him.

"Her husband has full confidence in her and lacks nothing of value. She brings him good and not harm, all the days of her life."

—Proverbs: 31: 11

Merry
Christmas
from
The
Daggetts

Chapter 8
Dark Daze

"God never promises to remove us from our struggles. He does promise, however, to change the way we look at them."

—Max Lucado

"When you think you've lost everything and life doesn't matter, God whispers I am still here."

—Alex Daggett

We have normalized using the word depression in nearly any context. Sometimes it is someone saying, "I feel down and depressed today." Other times it is an expression used after watching the news, "Wow, that is depressing." Prolonged bad weather can even be described as "depressing." It has made its way into conversation by celebrities, actors, athletes, counselors. Even pastors talk about it from a Biblical perspective.

I believe our son dealt with clinical depression and that the marijuana only exacerbated the problem. Through the past several years, I have had conversations with professionals, doctors, health nurses, parole officers, therapists, and police officers. My question to them at some point in the conversation is, "Why is there so much mental illness and depression?" Their answer every time is, "Drugs."

Marijuana is a gateway drug and then a progression to harder drugs, mind altering drugs. My personal conclusion, after spending considerable time with professionals in this field of study, is that if a person has even a small part of a disorder or condition, drugs can amplify the symptoms.

Some people claim that marijuana is not a gateway drug, but from my own research and from what I have observed and learned over the past several years, it is. The facts speak the hard truth. That does not mean that everyone who tries drugs will become an addict or mentally ill. Not everyone who goes to the casino becomes addicted to gambling, and not all people who drink alcohol are alcoholics. But I am quite sure we all know someone who has gone down the wrong path and gotten caught in the mire of addiction.

The more our son used drugs, the more he tried to "self-medicate," as he would say, the harder he spiraled down into a dark mentally challenging place. Navigating this devastating chapter in our lives took many years. And yes, it wasn't only our son's story, it was ours as well. Addiction is a family disease, we have learned. There are too many stories of heartbreak, crisis, and trials that I simply cannot share.

Some details are too complicated and unbearable to put on paper. There were months when we were left hanging in the balance of fear and hope, trauma and crisis. The worst was when our son started calling us from jail, a situation that repeated itself more than we care to admit. We would have so many unanswered questions as to how and why he ended up there. He collectively spent several months in jail over the span of four to five years. We would helplessly watch him isolate and explode with anger before turning back to drugs. Hearing he was in jail, again, we didn't know how to navigate the fear, shame, and uncertainty that we faced.

Greg was incarcerated for four Christmases in a row. At one point, two days before Christmas, he was sentenced to two years plus a day in prison. It was unthinkable and unimaginable for us as a family and as his parents. This was during the uncertain years of COVID-19, which made it feel even harder to face. He was initially sent to prison in Nova Scotia before being sent back to Dorchester in New Brunswick to complete his sentence. I am still haunted by the unknowns and lingering questions that threatened me during this terrible time.

My personal story of depression is different from my son's and was brought on by several occurrences from 2010 to 2019. Although it is very hard, I want to be vulnerable and share my story. Dealing with ongoing situations with my son, as well as facing my own battles, complicated and worsened the depression. The constant strain of managing Greg's fate, combined with my struggle to confront my own personal demons, intensified the effects of my own depression.

I was always a glass-half-full kind of person, then I progressed to the glass being empty, to the point of Where is the glass, I can't even find it? Dark days, or as I now call them "dark daze," melded into weeks, months, and years. It was a terrifying roller coaster ride of extreme lows and barely any highs. Did his out-of-control behavior affect me? Of course it did! As I was dealing with my own darkness, his situation added insult to injury. Do I blame him or think he was the root cause of my depression? No, I don't, but his actions sure did fuel the fire at times.

In 2003, I was diagnosed with viral pericarditis, inflammation of the pericardium, the sac that surrounds and protects the heart, caused by a viral infection. I had a very tough couple of years coping with that. I eventually weaned down the steroid I was taking and started to feel better both physically and mentally. From 2010 and on for a few years, I went through several different trials that would wear me down. I had to change careers after losing my business. At home, our adult children faced their own obstacles. Our older daughter moved her family to Alberta while the younger daughter was experiencing a new normal because of a marriage separation (and later divorce). We lost Joanne's parents, my beloved in-laws. My health problems brought their own troubles with medication side-effects and meeting with several doctors. In the end, this culminated in the loneliest time of my life. Greg, our prodigal son who had not yet returned to us, aggravated these feelings leading to many sleepless nights from the extra stress and worry, aggravating my health conditions. From that dark window of time in my life I wondered if there would ever be light at the end of the blackest tunnel.

I battled this way for many long days, nights, weeks, and into months. From 2018 until the spring of 2019, I fell into the deepest stages of depression. Usually, men don't admit to this vulnerability. They keep it to themselves to maintain a lie of invulnerability. But that lie imprisoned me even further into isolation and loneliness. As a Christian man, I experienced guilt and shame for feeling this way, which made it all worse. During the early months of 2019, I allowed myself to slip into many negative thoughts as I wrestled mentally to show a solid front as a man who should be able to carry his family's burdens with God's strength. It is very hard now to look back on that dark period.

1 Corinthians 13:13 speaks of faith, hope, and love. At that time in 2019, I barely hung onto my faith. I had wells of love for my wife and family, but sadly my own hope was gone. Without hope, we are in big trouble. I didn't even realize it was gone until I finally reached out to my wife, counselor, doctor, and friends (all of whom God had placed in my way when I was ready to let Him help me). I had lost hope for my son who was in jail (again) and saw no answers to my prayers in regard to his situation. I felt exhausted and overwhelmed from my health concerns, and all of these ongoing trials.

March of 2019 was a turning point. I realized I needed to seek help. I firmly believe the prayers of others kept me alive every day. I cannot go into the details of that day in March, one I will never forget, but I had left a note for my wife and children and had planned to end my life. What happened to me between writing the words and turning to Joanne, will stay between myself and God. Thankfully, I am still here.

I opened up to my wife who knew I was in a bad place but had no idea how truly bad it was. Then I admitted my intentions to our Christian counselor, and she walked me through my healing journey. My doctor gave me medication so that I could manage through the next year. He was a tremendous help. It took years to be able to be honest with my friends and family. The hardest part was telling my beautiful daughters and their husbands (as our youngest had found a wonderful new love), but I wanted them all to know the truth so we could support one another.

I believe drugs, mental illness, and suicide are the real epidemics in our nation today. People are talking more openly about them, but the crises continue. It makes me very upset every time I hear of another suicide. It affects whole families and even communities. Too many beautiful souls have left this earth as they just couldn't cope with life anymore. It is beyond tragic.

This is why I tell my story. If I can help even one person, it will be worth it all. Although all the details of my story are too deeply personal to share here, I still feel the need to write down what is important so that someone else's hope might come back to them.

"Even though I walk through the darkest valley I will fear no evil for you are with me."

—Psalm 23:4

Chapter 9
Boundaries and Enabling

"Drawing boundaries can help put out fires before they become all consuming. But if the fire keeps burning with increasing intensity, you've got to get away from the smoke and flames. Sometimes your only option is to say goodbye."

—Lysa TerKeurst

"Completely letting go of your child and letting God take over is one of the hardest things a parent can do."

—Alex Daggett

Boundaries and *enabling* are two topics my wife and I had to learn about. We read books, saw a counselor, attended courses hosted by our government funded support agency, Ridgewood Addiction and Mental Health Services. We talked with other couples walking a similar road as us, to try and glean as much knowledge as we could. We learned helpful answers to questions like: *How do I keep myself healthy? Am I enabling my son by doing certain things for him? What boundaries should I enforce that are fair, good, Christian? What changes do I need to make, or adjust to depending on the current circumstances?* It was a challenging time trying to navigate these deep waters and to implement new, but necessary, ideas.

An "enabler" is defined by Cambridge dictionary (based on a psychological premise) as "someone who allows or makes it possible for another person to behave in a way that damages that person." From my experience, it is the action of helping (or making it possible and easy for) a loved one to continue to do the same thing over and over. Maybe it looks like paying their bills, giving them money often to avoid confrontation about their addiction or destructive behavior. It could also look like letting them get away with unwanted actions, or damaging conduct, and never saying no. Joanne and I have read several books that deal with this problem.

Our list:

- *Addict in the Family: Stories of Loss, Hope and Recovery* by Beverly Conyers.

- *Don't Let Your Kids Kill You: A Guide for Parents of Drug and Alcohol Addicted Children* by Charles Rubin.

- *Good Boundaries and Goodbyes: Loving Others without Losing the Best of Who You Are* by Lysa TerKeurst.

All these books focus on the consequences of enabling

and providing strategies on how to set boundaries. They are so informative, filled with truths that can help parents and loved ones. When I was younger and learning to drive, my father told me, "You do the crime, you pay the time." I find that parenting today means bailing kids out of their own consequences of their negative actions.

Now, if anyone understands this and realizes how hard it is to say no, it's me. How many lies did I just ignore? How much deception could I have endured? How many times did I bail him out of a financial jamb? How could he have continued to live with us when trust and respect were nonexistent?

In her book, Lysa Terkeurst says, "We must not confuse the good commands to love and forgive with the bad realities of enabling and covering up things that are not honoring to God."[2] Wow! That really hit me hard and triggered many memories.

As a parent you want to help and support your child, especially if they are healthy and trying to improve their life. But what if they are making unhealthy choices that lead to addiction, acting out of control, and taking you down with them? It is impossible to try and have a healthy relationship with an unhealthy person, while continuing to enable them to live out their lifestyle. It will wear you out, bring you down, cause marriage issues, conflict with other siblings, cause health issues and yes, it could eventually kill you.

The definition of insanity is "Doing the same thing over and over again but expecting a different result." (Rita Mae Brown) When we enable someone to continue their bad choices and help them out repeatedly, it is a bit insane! Yes, people *can* change. Even Kenny Chesney reminded us in one of his songs "Some people change." But the sad truth is that many don't. I am pretty sure that most

---

[2] TerKeurst, L. (2022). *Good Boundaries and Goodbyes* (p. 4). Thomas Nelson.

addicts, no matter what the addiction is, *want to change*, but are controlled by the powerful claws of addiction.

Years ago, Joanne and I attended a three-day course on addiction and enabling the addict. We listened and watched as many parents, couples, families, and loved ones shared. One couple were in their late sixties and still had their forty-five-year-old alcoholic son living in their basement. They broke down weeping as they told their story of the countless times, they had actually bailed their son out of jail, given him a place to live, given him money, paid for multiple rehabilitation center stays, all while thinking, *This will be the last time*.

After they listened to the rest of the group and gained valuable information at the sessions, they both admitted, "We can't do this anymore; it is going to kill us." However, that is easier said than done. We are always thinking that today is the day for true change. As parents we long for that change, hope and pray for it too, but it doesn't always work out the way we want it to.

Well-meaning people would often offer to me, "He just needs to hit rock bottom." My response? "He *has* hit rock bottom. A *number* of times." He has lost his wife and children to his addiction. He has been kicked out of rental units to live on the streets and in and out of shelters. He has been jailed and imprisoned. He has left us wondering if he was alive or dead because we hadn't heard from him for so long. Yes, *rock bottom* was a reality for him and a nightmare for us. Of course, we had tried talking to him privately. We tried family interventions. We tried counseling, begging, pleading, crying, fighting, and even silence, but to no avail. I am so thankful for praying, supportive friends and family who have walked with us and given us words of kindness and wisdom.

There were also sincere people during this time who said some foolish and hurtful things. Words like, "Don't worry; he will come around." Or the classic, "Just pray more and have more faith." Another hurtful comment was "Your son must have had a tough childhood." But the one that really stuck with me and hit hardest was, "Just let go and let God." Yes, okay true, but also too blunt and harsh. Those words can wound an already bleeding heart. One lady said that to me and her husband spoke up and asked her, "Could you do that with one of our kids? Just let go and let God?"

The hard fact is I have had to "let God" over the past several years, and it is a difficult, daily handing-over progression. Some days are not as hard, but others are extremely difficult. Letting go means I am trusting God no matter what happens today, tomorrow, or next year. I am doing better with that most days. Setting up boundaries and not enabling are crucial to living a healthy life and surviving amid the challenges.

Does Jesus really want me to set up boundaries? Isn't it loving and Christian to always be there for someone no matter how they treat or mistreat you? No, it's not. And Jesus didn't ever want anyone to be used wrongly, abused verbally or physically or attacked by bad behavior over and over again. My Christian counselor helped me through this process and to realize that we need healthy boundaries. She gave us scriptures and examples of what Jesus did with those who did not like nor agree with him and even those who wanted to kill him.

At one counseling session, after expressing how hard it was to set boundaries, my counselor asked, "Alex, would you let anyone else use you this way? Say hurtful things to your wife? Control and upset you all the time and lie to you over and over again?"

Of course, I immediately replied, "No!"

"That's why you need boundaries."

I realized then that it was *my responsibility* to change

the way things were. I had had enough of my son's abusive verbal attacks. Even though Greg would push back against them, I knew boundaries were going to benefit me.

Even after all this time, it is painful to write these words, to relive the memories of hurt and disappointment. It seems to me that this kind of grief never gets easier to bear. I continue to ask, *Why, Lord, why? What is the good in all this as You promised?* The questions and thoughts play in my head over and over.

Initially, I did set some boundaries and then gradually implemented more and more. I blocked his number after repeated verbal and frightening attacks on our family. I set limitations on when he could come to our home. He was not permitted to engage in ignorant and abusive behavior of which we had zero tolerance. We would not visit him if he used drugs. Absolutely no money was given if he acted in an out-of-control manner. These boundaries evolved over the years according to our current situation and our son's status.

Enforcing boundaries is extremely difficult. It is harder on the hearts and minds of parents. It can feel devastating, heart-wrenching, unthinkable, and unreal. It is hard to comprehend how we arrived at this place in our lives.

Our boundaries with Greg were easier to adhere to when he was in jail or prison. Jail?!? *How did we get here?* In one sense, it was easier knowing he was off the streets and unable to hurt himself or anyone else. On the other hand, accepting this as our son's reality was too painful. Worse, this knowledge was not secret. Again, the ambivalent comments arose while I was in my darkest struggle. A man at church one Sunday morning said to me;

"Well at least it is good he is in jail, you know where he is for a while."

Wow, really, did I just hear that? I didn't even know

how to respond, but my mind was raged. *That is the dumbest thing anyone has said to me yet.* I felt like asking him how he would feel if *his* son was in jail. These thoughtless comments felt like a gut-punch. The Rock, Dwayne Johnson, said "Setting boundaries with draining people doesn't mean you don't love them. It just means you love yourself too."

"Do not associate with one easily angered, or you may learn their ways and get yourself ensnared."

—Proverbs 22:24

Chapter 10
Trauma

"Major trauma can create emotional disruption."

—Dr. Phil

"Trauma is the hidden pain that can resurface at any time again and again."

—Alex Daggett

I miss my dad and his wisdom. My wife and I just visited our island home, Grand Manan, for the Canada Day long weekend. It is hard for me to visit my mom's house knowing my dad isn't there anymore. His absence rings loud in my ears. I see his chair, his tools, his Bible and beloved books, but I miss seeing him. I am thankful for many wonderful memories, but there are also so many triggers on the island that take me back to thoughts of my dad and son.

Our little village and church, the beaches, the cottage at Miller Pond, our house where love and family lived, the school, the ballfield and swimming pool are all reminders of days gone by. Good days with laughter, fun, and family gatherings. Days when our son was healthy, and life was busy but less stressful and so much easier. Driving through our little village of Seal Cove brings flashbacks to another time and many fond memories that live on in my heart.

Triggers can be both good and bad. The hard hurtful ones can lead to trauma. Just when you think you have forgotten or blocked out a painful situation, it rears its ugly head again. I'm not sure if trauma or triggers ever go away because I've been living with them for almost twenty years now.

Joanne and I find it difficult to drive into certain parts of a nearby city, where our son lived in run-down apartments or on the streets. It is hard to fully explain just how this made us feel and how being there still brings back feelings of stress, fear, sadness, anger, and anxiety. We would find ourselves looking for him on every corner or in an alley, and it was like every hopeless, nameless face we saw was like seeing our own son again. I would think, *That is someone's daughter, son, father, mother, sister, friend.* My wife wrote this poem.

Somebody's Son

I wonder as I walk
Why is this my story?
How is this our story?
I wonder
I saw him as I walked toward
the grocery store
He played a melody on a drum
standing in the freezing sunshine
on a bitter February morning
alone
And I thought to myself
I'll give him some money on my way out
yes, on my way out
praying I wouldn't forget
We all passed him by
busy mothers, grey haired grandmas
rushing truck drivers
all of us busy with our busy lives
I wondered did any of us notice?
On my way out I started reaching
for my wallet and the cash
I'd been saving
for the perfect opportunity to use it
in this debit-cashless-tap and go-world
I KNEW this was the moment
and I gently laid the money
in his navy knitted hat

He now sat on the icy cold snow
maybe he was tired
of being tired
In that moment my eyes met his
and I memorized his face
words formed on my lips
but didn't escape my mouth
I turned to go with a small wave
-not enough!
oh, not nearly enough I thought
and I turned
and locked eyes with him again
until tears started leaking out of my eyes and down
my frozen cheeks
A voice in my head screamed
he's somebody's brother
uncle
father
friend
grandson
son
He is somebody's son
sitting alone
beating a melody on a drum
alone
On my walk I wonder
What is his story?
Why is my story mine?
Maybe so I can see things
more clearly
differently

than I ever did before
through a heavenly lens
I hear my Abba
the Beautiful One whisper
it's ok to let tears leak out of your eyes
it's ok to be human
it's ok
And I breathe a prayer
in the freezing February sunshine
for somebody's son

⚜

Even now, we are hesitant to enter that area of the city, even if invited to go to a restaurant with friends. To be frank, we avoid it if at all possible.

For years when an unfamiliar phone number came up on our phones, we would imagine the worst—a voice saying they had found our son somewhere. When the police would drive by our home at the end of our street, we assumed the worst—*Was he arrested? Did they find him beat up? Dead?* These thoughts, seemingly irrational or silly to others, were a result of years of experiencing crisis and trauma.

As Jane Leavy, American sportswriter and biographer, wrote, "Trauma fractures comprehension as a pebble shatters a windshield. The wound at the site of impact spreads across the field of vision, obscuring reality and challenging belief."

There are songs, movies, shows, and even local radio news stations that I won't watch or listen to. The morning news would report on an arrest, and I would pause to listen for our son's name. It is a terrible experience for a father's heart. Trauma became an acronym for me:

*T*ry

*R*esisting

*A*ll

*U*r

*M*ind

*A*llows

Many things can trigger trauma for me—a father and

son hanging out or playing sports together, even working on a project together.

Just a few weeks before I wrote this paragraph, Joanne and I were on a beautiful beach, enjoying the sunshine while reading and enjoying each other's company. Behind us sat two younger women. After a while, one began playing a few tunes on her guitar, humming along as she plucked the strings. It was lovely, not too loud, pleasant to the ear. Instantly my mind went to our son, who was a great guitar player. I thought of a particular song he would play. It produced simultaneous feelings of joy and mourning. A fond memory of him playing, and grief that he no longer picks up a guitar. We loved singing along with him while he played. Now the guitar is still. The instrument is silent, and the player doesn't sing.

Later on that evening, I had asked Joanne what she thought when she heard the girl playing guitar at the beach. I knew she had been listening too. Her instant reply was, "I thought it was nice, but then I thought of Greg, and it hurt." Trauma caused those feelings. It wasn't a guy playing the guitar. The young lady wasn't sitting beside us asking for requests or even playing a familiar song, but we both had the same gut-punch reaction.

Watching our son's children, our grandchildren, grow, there are many triggers for us there. The ways they talk, look, laugh, joke around, and even what they are interested in remind us of our son. It is almost uncanny how much our grandson moves and acts like our son did at that same age. We notice all the similar things our grandson likes to do. He enjoys being silly and making us laugh. He likes to play outside, and then inside on video games. He has a keen mind and loves to ask us funny, interesting questions to make us think and laugh. He is always humming a tune, like Greg used to do. Our granddaughter's features take after Greg. She is creative, artsy, and full of fun. We love having them spend time with us, and they still think we are cool. Processing the reality that they have a new home with a new dad is challenging for us, even though we are very thankful for those provisions. Thinking about what "could have been" is a trigger for sadness, more than it is trauma.

For me, trauma and grief are similar in that they can both knock me off balance when I am not expecting it. Seeing certain people, smelling something, driving by a tent city, hearing a familiar song of a time gone by, seeing a person holding up a sign looking for money, reading a post on Facebook or a news article about drugs, prison, homelessness, etc., all evoke trauma for me. I crawl into bed at night, close my eyes, and there it is again.

Only by the grace of God can I turn this over to Him each day and pray that He carries me through another day. Only God knows my heart, has listened to my rants in the truck while I pound on the steering wheel, has watched me pace back and forth in the house with anger and hurt boiling up inside me, has heard me ask so many questions, who has been silent at times yet always there. He has forgiven me time and time again when I don't show the fruits of the Spirit. Trauma can make you or break you, like many challenges in life. It can make you bitter or better.

Thank you, Lord, for forgiving me countless times and for helping me deal with all the triggers and trauma. Tomorrow is another new day that I must give over to you again and place my trust in You, for the things I can't see, control, or change.

"Come to me, all you who are weary and burdened, and I will give you rest."

—Matthew 11:28

Chapter 11

Reap What We Sow: Society Today

"With so many things coming back in style, I can't wait until morals, respect and intelligence become a trend again."

—Danilo Portella

"Common sense now seems to be a relative term that people use for their own agenda."

—Alex Daggett

When I reflect upon our current social state, I am appalled. At the time of writing, I turned 58, and a span of time that has afforded me a front-row seat to a multitude of societal shifts. There have been so many, in fact, that the world around me often feels unreal. Life, by design, changes continuously. While some of these changes are undoubtedly positive, many others are so profound that they are difficult to fully comprehend.

Just four decades ago, I walked across the stage at my high school graduation. The world I inhabit now is vastly different from the one I knew then with the most obvious movement being our reliance on the use of computers, internet, social media, and smartphones. It seems that everything is recorded, uploaded, and judged. Forty years may seem like a mere blip on the radar of history, but an unbelievable amount of transformation can occur within that time frame.

Additionally, I am shocked at the lack of common sense. I was having a conversation with my brother a few weeks ago, and he reminded me, "Common sense sure isn't very common now, and as a matter of fact, do we even know what common sense is?" He was right! What used to be common sense for most people isn't that common now. There are so many different beliefs and ideologies out there that each group believes that they have the most common sense. Dr. Phil said, "Common sense needs to be more common."

Years ago, I remember reading a quote from James Dobson, then president of Focus on the Family, a fundamentalist Protestant organization. He said, "Those who control what young people are taught, and what they experience, what they see, hear, think, and believe will determine the future course of our nation." He was right and predicted what was coming for our society.

My dad said similar things like that as well. He would

recall his younger years and all the changes he had seen as I am doing now. Dad would say, "As we continue to take God and the church out of everything, we will pay for it in the future." Or, "It's a slippery slope we're (society) heading down as we remove God from each area of our life."

I learned from my father, who didn't say he belonged to a religion, but was a Christian man who believed in the Holy Trinity (the Father, the Son, and the Holy Spirit) and who lived by faith. This always interested me and as I matured, I understood this more clearly. It is grace and faith that I believe in, too.

Although there seems to be so many religions now, thousands have existed for at least hundreds of years. So, what is different? The birth of generic or superficial religions is a result of the enormity of people connecting over the internet and justifying their "religion" for whatever purpose they want. It doesn't take much to create a website/social media ID. Just because something is done in the name of God (or any named "higher power") doesn't mean it is good for mankind.

Our son has a beautiful, keen mind that was suppressed by the demons of drugs and alcohol. I was excited to think that someday he would use it as he studied for his Master of Arts in Theology. He had a passion to learn and explore different cultures, beliefs, and religions. I knew he would be awesome! I could see him as a teacher or professor, debating ideas with other bright young minds. That dream, however, became a nightmare. His mind was irreparably damaged by his experimentation with mind-altering drugs. This prevented him from ever realizing his ambition to teach and share his knowledge with others. Why? How does this make sense? We may never know the answer.

1 Peter 5:8 teaches us that the enemy, Satan, prowls

around to seek and destroy what is good. I believe that is what happened to my son as the "enemy" tried to destroy not only Greg's life, but also mine, my wife's, my children, and Greg's family. With no answers for this mystery, I simply have to put my trust in Him.

I passed a billboard sign that read, "Before we work anymore on artificial intelligence, why don't we do something about natural stupidity and no common sense." Cannabis was recreationally and medically legalized in 2018. Although the *Cannabis Act* has "several measures that help prevent youth from accessing marijuana," in my opinion, the passing of this law was a huge mistake without being rooted in common sense.[3] Since the Canadian government (and thus our society) has granted permission for legal drug use, our kids interpret the message that said drug use is acceptable. After all, it is legally sold at the local store in many enticing, edible and inviting forms.

Even though not everyone who smokes pot is going to become addicted or spiral deep down into homelessness, we have to ask, "What is next?" I tremble to think what toxic road we pave with our laws. I have seen the socially accepted use of *illegal* drugs everywhere. I have read about the numbers of those dying—yes, dying—by overdose, and it doesn't matter that the Canadian government has "committed over $1 billion...to address the illegal toxic drug and overdose crisis" since 2017.[4] Survivors' lives are ruined and that impacts their friends and families.

Sometimes it takes years to recover from addiction. And sometimes, the consequences are darker. "Opioids were present in 61% of poisoning hospitalizations among

---

[3] *Cannabis Legalization And Regulation.* (n.d.). Government of Canada. Retrieved February 16, 2025, from https://www.justice.gc.ca/eng/cj-jp/cannabis/

[4] Government of Canada. (2024, December). *Federal actions on the overdose crisis.* https://www.canada.ca/en/health-canada/services/opioids/federal-actions/overview.html

people experiencing homelessness."[5] Although this does not prove those who are unhoused are so because of drugs, it does prove that illegal drug use is rampant in unsheltered communities.

Yet, there is always hope as long as there is faith. When I give $5 or $10 out of my truck window to a panhandler at a busy intersection, I look them in the eyes. Friends will ask me why I donate, knowing my background and views. A few have even retorted that they won't give a cent; they would just tell them to get a job. My reply is, "Well, you don't know them, their story, or what they may have been through." My $5 could be their next step back to a better life. I give that to God and pray about the rest.

Many adults who end up on the streets aren't criminals who grew up in bad neighborhoods or unloving homes. It is wholly possible that they aren't living this way by choice or acceptance. Most have experienced hardship or crisis that led to their situations. Anyone is susceptible. By publicly accepting drugs into the mainstream, they have risen to become the greatest epidemic against our society.

A study in the Drug and Alcohol Dependence Reports found that "[d]rug overdose deaths among adults 65 years of age and older in Canada rose from 4.3 to 9.9 deaths per million in the entire population between 2000 and 2022." Additionally, "[d]rug overdose deaths more than doubled in Canada and opioid overdose deaths more than tripled in Ontario among adults 65 years of age and older during the past two decades."[6] Drug use and abuse worsens daily and impacts across all age groups. We are reaping what we have sown.

---

[5] Government of Canada. (2021, June 23). *Substance-related poisonings and homelessness in Canada: a descriptive analysis of hospitalization data.* https://www.canada.ca/en/health-canada/services/opioids/hospitalizations-substance-related-poisonings-homelessness.html

[6] Imtiaz, S., Ali, F., Kaminski, N., Russell, C., & Rehm, J. (2024). Trends in drug overdose deaths among adults 65 years of age and older in Canada (2000–2022). *Drug and Alcohol Dependence Reports, 12*, 100254. https://doi.org/10.1016/j.dadr.2024.100254

Dad, you were right what you said years ago. Now my children and my grandchildren are seeing a whole new world and society, without God our Creator in the middle of it because we keep taking Him out of more things.

"Whoever sows to please their flesh, from the flesh will reap destruction, whoever sows to please the spirit, from the spirit will reap eternal life."

—Galatians 6:8

Chapter 12

Why Write?

"Do what you have to do, to do what you want to do."

—Denzel Washington

When God prompts you to do something, pay attention, and get ready for the journey.

—Alex Daggett

Years ago, I set about journaling on a regular basis. I stopped after three years and looked back at my writings, only to realize how dark and depressing they were. I threw them all out. Although the process of writing did help me through that time in my life, I knew I didn't want anyone else to read my painful journey.

So, why write now? I had to contemplate answering it over the past few months. I feel God has laid it on my heart to tell my story. Our story. God's story. It is not easy to say yes to something that requires me to be so vulnerable. The writing process also requires a lot of extra time. I watched my wife when she opened up to God and wrote her own testimony three years ago. She also said yes to God, and He has used her poems, prayers, and prose to touch many readers.

Denying God is so much easier than giving in to what He wants you to do. I didn't feel right. He wanted me to expose my pain and anguish. He wanted me to commit my son's story to a public audience. He wanted me to reopen the raw scars of my past. But really, God had asked me to write my truth, one that could offer hope. After a few months of struggling between my inner voice and God's omniscient voice, I sat down on a random Sunday afternoon in May, and began. I told Joanne what I was going to do. She encouraged me to try and see where the words would take me. And even though the path was uneven, cold, and lonely, she knew God would lead me in what to write. After all, if God is for us, who can be against us?

I write to encourage others who are dealing with their own prodigal child who, like ours, has yet to return home despite the countless offers to help. The "child" who has lost control of their lives to addiction. The "child" who abandoned the love and support of friends, family and faith. The "child" who lacks resources to aid in combating dependency, mental illness, and/or homelessness.

Kay Warren's book, *Choose Joy: Because Happiness isn't Enough,* details her son's struggle with mental illness and his eventual suicide. This news was deeply shocking to me. Despite Rick Warren's position as a pastor and the couple's efforts to seek counseling and prayers for their son, he tragically succumbed to his demons.

Their experience mirrored ours in many ways, leading me to question God's purpose in allowing such suffering. It seemed unfathomable that a couple so dedicated to ministry and helping others would lose their son. I still struggle with this lack of understanding.

Warren's book, which I've read twice, has been instructive. Beyond its lessons, I am most inspired by her unwavering faith amidst her questions. Despite the immense grief, she continues to choose joy and persevere.

Some things on this side of heaven will never be understood nor explained.

I know there are so many dealing with ongoing crises, addiction, and/or mental illnesses within what should be the safety net of family. Some parents or family members try to hide the problem or refuse to ask for help or prayer because of shame, guilt, hurt, or pride. I get it! I've been there several times, and those confusing feelings can consume your life. If you are dealing with this, I would suggest you try to find a friend or someone you can confide in that is trustworthy and who you can share openly with. Get counseling if you can. Share with a small group. Open up, if possible, as this will help you and your loved one.

The news of another opioid overdose or drug-related suicide is enough to make me think there are bodies on city streets of major Canadian cities. From 2016 to 2024, nearly 50,000 "apparent opioid toxicity deaths" were reported.[7]   It is overwhelming and heartbreaking. Drug abuse, overdoses, and suicide affect individuals from all walks of life, not just a specific group.

I have listened to Christian artist Toby Mac's music for years, and I enjoy his songs and lyrics that boldly proclaim his faith. He is such a talented songwriter! However, in the last few years, I can hear the undertones of his raw grief and heartache in a number of his current songs. Toby Mac's son, Truett, died from an accidental overdose of fentanyl and amphetamines in 2019. The entire music world was in shock. If I'd had the chance, I would have hugged both the artist and his wife, Amanda. I have the utmost respect for him and his resilience to press forward through his grief and pain. I thank him for being a role model to me. I will listen to his song, "Help is on the way," nearly every day. The verse that hits me the hardest is: "Sometimes it's days, sometimes it's years, some face a lifetime of fallen tears."[8] I realize the truth of this as I reflect on the journey of the last twenty years with Greg. It feels raw and real as I sit surrounded by unanswered prayers.

I find encouragement and hope in a wide variety of music genres, including country, gospel, worship, hymns, classical, pop, and rock. Music has always played a significant role in my life. After all, I was a teenager in the eighties, so I grew up with many great bands, but I also sang beloved familiar hymns in our little Baptist church. I even stretched out to the wild side and started singing contemporary worship songs, but not ones too upbeat or rock and roll.

Our son loved music too, and it was a huge part of his life. It breaks me that it doesn't matter to him anymore.

---

[7] Public Health of Canada, & Government of Canada. (2024, December 23). *Key Findings: Opioid- And Stimulant-related Harms In Canada — Canada.ca*. https://health-infobase.canada.ca/substance-related-harms/opioids-stimulants/

[8] TobyMac. (2021, February 19). Help Is On The Way (Maybe Midnight). In *Help Is On The Way (Maybe Midnight) - Single*. https://music.apple.com/us/album/help-is-on-the-way-maybe-midnight/1553371777?i=1553371780

While visiting with him a few months ago, I asked him if we could get him a guitar (as his others were long gone), and he just said no. That shook me. He used to love to play, sing, make up silly and fun songs, while entertaining young and old alike.

Greg is just one of many who have abandoned their gifts to dependency. The loss of a life unfulfilled due to drug abuse, overdose, and mental illness among those my age and younger infuriates and saddens me. The list of those impacted is extensive—too extensive.

How can this situation be fixed? How can we make a difference? By being there to listen, offering unwavering love, and praying for them, we can support others one person at a time. Mother Teresa has many quotes, but one specifically that resonates with me:

"I used to pray that God would feed the hungry, or do this or that, but now I pray that He will guide me to do whatever I'm supposed to do, what I can do. I used to pray for answers, but now I'm praying for strength. I used to believe that prayer changes things, but now I know that prayer changes us, and we change things."

I am no Mother Teresa, but I write my words with prayer. I write to be real and raw, to encourage someone and to hopefully make a difference to whoever needs it today or tomorrow.

"Though the mountains be shaken and the hills be removed, yet my unfailing love for you will not be shaken nor my covenant of peace be removed."

—Isaiah 54:10

Joanne, Greg , Holly, Alex and Marissa

Chapter 13

A Story

"People are dying to be listened to. People are dying to be able to pour out their hearts and not be judged. Not be told their crazy, not be told their feelings don't matter."

—Kay Warren

"Be careful how you treat each person as you don't know their story and what they are dealing with."

—Alex Daggett

Just about everyone has a story of loss, heartache, crisis, shattered dreams, and unthinkable difficulties. You may be greeted by someone who speaks a friendly hello or good morning but may have had a terrible night or week that you will likely never know about. I've read and heard firsthand accounts of unbelievably hard, hurtful, stories and the comebacks people have had even when up against the wall.

One of my favorite books is, *The Happiest Man on Earth: The Beautiful Life of an Auschwitz Survivor* by Eddie Jaku, a Jew and Holocaust survivor who revealed the incredible story of all he endured.[9] I'll admit that it was challenging to read as certain parts of the story were gut-wrenching to even imagine what happened to him and so many other imprisoned Jews. Against all odds, Jaku survived. Later in life he married, had children and grandchildren. He rediscovered love, life, and laughter. He celebrated his 100th birthday in 2020 and died the following year. He turned his horrible past into a positive and beautiful life and that, too, is a powerful legacy.

So why does my story matter? Mine doesn't seem anywhere as significant as Jaku's. But it doesn't have to be. God made us in His image to be our own unique selves, with original tales to share. They are reflective of how we exist in the world. My story matters because I matter. And your story matters, too, for the same reason.

I love learning other people's stories and narratives, their experiences, accomplishments, and lessons learned. Perhaps he overcame a tough start and went on to bravely make a new life. I think most people enjoy hearing "comeback" stories. Those stories matter. I am a sports nut and love watching all kinds of different sports. Maybe that is why I liked Wayne Gretzky's book, *99: Stories of the*

---

9 Jaku, E. (2022). *Happiest Man on Earth*. Pan Books.

Game.[10] I like how humble and classy he is. He was told for years that he'd be too small in size to play professional hockey, but he became one of the greatest players ever.

The story that I love best is the one I share with my wife. Hanging above our bed, we have a large, framed quote that says, "My favorite love story is ours." Thirty-seven years of us, being one, doing life together with Jesus at the center.

This is where the story deviates in several ways. When Joanne and I started seeing each other again we were nineteen and twenty-years old, respectively. We began married life with a baby boy along for the journey. I remember looking down at him many times when he was an infant and wondering, *What will your story be? You've been gifted to me. How will God use you later in life? Were your mom and I brought back together for a reason?* I pondered these questions and ideas over and over as the years pressed on.

We taught our three children about God and Jesus. Our faith was a central part of our life and home. We were not perfect parents nor have the perfect marriage, but we tried to model and show God to them through our everyday lives. Proverbs 22:6 states, "Start children off on the way they should go, and even when they are old, they will not turn from it." A simple straightforward yet profound verse, it has come to my mind many times over the last thirty years. Even more so in the last ten years. I thought for sure my talented, smart, gifted, and blessed son was destined to be used by God in some way. He loved working with kids and spent every summer going to an island camp on the Saint John River. Each year he would be given more responsibility and, therefore, he would spend more time there. By the time he was in high school most of his summer was spent working at this camp. We have heard so many stories over the years from parents

10 Gretzky, W. (2016). *99: Stories of the Game.* Penguin.

and kids of how much they loved Greg, how much fun he was, and how he would play games with them, and play his guitar at the evening campfires. Even the camp director shared with us how much he appreciated Greg, his work ethic, and how well he engaged with the other counselors and campers. We were thankful he had this wonderful opportunity to work there and enjoy his summers as God used him in this way.

Near that period of time, when he was about twenty, is when things went sideways. We knew something wasn't right as we watched our son make devastating choices. Then after a couple of years, he seemed to be doing better before leaving for university for four years. Then he proceeded to complete two additional years of Divinity college, got married and had a baby on the way. There are a hundred untold stories during that period that I cannot disclose as they are both devastating to recount and I believe not mine to tell. Unfortunately, the story became a train wreck that kept going off the tracks time and time again, derailing both his family and ours. Here is where I've asked God questions like how did we get here, and what is the purpose for all of this?

I don't like this part of my story, and it has been very hard to recall and think about as I write it down. I wonder again why this happened? Why was our son's mind destroyed in so many ways? Why has there been all this hurt and pain? I sit with the ache of unanswered questions, for now anyway. Maybe I will sit with these questions until I stand in Heaven.

When I watch other men working or hanging out or playing with their sons, it hurts. It hurts more than I can explain or put into words. I wish I could say that everything has worked out for the best, that a lot of healing has happened, and that my son is on a positive new path. Unfortunately, it never did work out that way. Not yet. Maybe it will. Maybe it never will. I don't know or understand. But I have to keep praying, believing, hoping and pressing on.

I know some stories are redemption stories and others are not. I have lived long enough to know that life is a very blessed thing, but it also comes with much grief and sorrow at times. I don't think you are quite ever the same person after you've experienced tragedy, trauma, or loss, but I have great respect for those who have learned to trust and believe in God in the middle of it all. These people matter to God who created us in His image.

"Therefore, as God's chosen people, holy and dearly loved, clothe yourselves with compassion, kindness, humility, gentleness and patience."

—Colossians 3:12

Chapter 14

Summertime

"I wonder what it would be like to live in a world where it was always June"

—L.M. Montgomery

"Oh the great memories and fun that summer holds for us."

—Alex Daggett

It is July as I sit here writing. I do love summer. I do love all the seasons for their own reasons, but summertime is my most anticipated favorite. Usually, summer is the season when the family comes home for a visit, and we enjoy quality time together. I have worked in construction most of my life, so I appreciate agreeable weather and temperature. I would rather be hot and looking for shade than be too cold and scrambling for heat.

Greg had loved the warmer season, too, from his time working with children at a summer camp. While on break from university, he would work for several weeks at my construction at job sites with me and my crew. Then, he would head off to the camp for the remainder of his time out of school. It was great having him with me since he got along so well with the crew. He fit in well and everyone treated him like part of the pack. Greg learned skills of the trade, but I knew in his heart that he was a bookworm, an intellect, and would be more scholar than tradesman. He excelled in his studies. He thought outside the box about many ideas and theories. The time away from school, at the camp or with us, was a way for him to give his mind a rest from studying and a chance to relax.

Of all his hobbies, skateboarding was Greg's favorite. He practiced and became quite skilled at it. He spent hours attempting a certain trick until he finally mastered it. When he was about fourteen, we built him a half-pipe ramp inside one of my large buildings. This allowed him and his friends to practice more no matter what the weather. But, when June rolled around, they were outside with plenty of sunshine and warm temps to kickflip, ollie, and boardslide. I can still hear their skateboards today, the clickity click and banging noises when someone wiped out.

I am not sure what summer means to him now, or if it holds any special meaning to him at all. Now his days all look the same and it would seem like summer would be no different than any other season. Summer for me now is a bittersweet reminder of what was.

Yesterday the sky radiated a beautiful blue with hardly any clouds. Joanne and I went kayaking. Boats of all types sailed around us. Everyone was enjoying a great afternoon on the river. Nothing quite relaxes me more than moments like this, with all of God's creation around me. No cell phones, no schedules, just relaxing with a paddle in my hands and a warm breeze on my back. Even then, a memory of Greg, our Greg before he disappeared into himself, will flood my mind, sending a winter chill up the back of my neck.

Summer holds the warm memories of family— birthdays, weddings, anniversaries, and family time at the camp by the pond. Both of our daughters were married during the summer. On one of those wedding days, a good friend lost his daughter in a car accident. I will never forget that day. How could I? I called that friend recently as that date approached, and we chatted. It amazes me that he will call and check in on me sometimes, too, even in the middle of his grief and pain.

This summer marks our 38th wedding anniversary, a milestone that is becoming rare. I am thankful and blessed each day and don't take for granted the great marriage we have. We are not claiming a perfect union by any means. We have been tested by fire many times. However, our ship has been guided by our Lord and Captain. My dad would often say, "It's the eighth wonder of the world when a couple can stay together for life and actually still like and love each other." I chuckled at that when I heard it, but now I understand.

Even though summer brings many great days and memories, it also carries ones I would rather not have. It was a summer day when our eighteen-year-old son packed up and left home and not on good terms. We offered to get him help, anywhere, but he refused and walked right out the door. For months we didn't know where he was or where he was living. We wondered: *How is he doing? Does he have a safe place to stay? Is he eating enough? Or worse, Is he still using drugs? Is he even alive?*

It may sound dramatic, but it was our reality of a volatile situation we were all living in. I wouldn't wish those days and painful questions on anyone. Penning these words is very emotional. Only by the grace of God, angels by his side, and the prayers of many people who love him, can we say he is alive today. There are countless untold stories of how God stood by his side, and ours, even in the dark shadowy places. Once, he told us a story of how he had walked quite a way to get to a ferry but had no money to pay the fare. A stranger saw that he was in need and paid his ticket. At another time, a woman at church had bought some shoes for him because she saw that he had none. There are no words to express our feelings on hearing these tales. We thank God that He watched over our son, but we are torn apart knowing that we could not help him in his time of need. We are reminded that we are not at fault for this, but it doesn't lessen the pain.

I am a simple blue-collar guy who happens to be a Red Seal carpenter. I am not a theologian nor a pastor. I do not consider myself highly intelligent nor the scripture-quoting kind of guy. I love building things with my hands. I love my wife and family. I have a heart for God and country and tend to view things in a less complicated way. Music and singing were always a big part of my life; in fact, my wife and I often sang together at church. However, when my heart and spirit became wounded, the music faded.

The moment he walked out of the house that summer was the start of a heart-wrenching, soul-searching, faith-testing, and life-pondering twenty-year journey. And that journey silently continues each day.

It has been over three weeks since I've written anything. Our daughter, her husband and their kids have been visiting with us. We have spent beautiful days splashing in the waves cresting on the sandy beaches that touch the ocean. Some afternoons, we played in the nearby river. One week was spent on Grand Manan Island, camping at our family's cottage at Miller Pond—a wonderful spot to swim, relax, boat, fish, and kayak. It was busy yet fun, tiring yet heart-filling, with lots of laughter, food, and hugs. My heart is renewed by the memories we made during those sunshine-filled days.

Staying there brought back memories of us spending countless days, nights through different seasons at this inviting, homey cottage. Our little rustic camp in the middle of the woods smelled of wood fires, homemade bread, and baked beans. It was a soft place to land. A red chimney puffed smoke, and the wide windows gave us a view of the little pond with ducks paddling by and eagles soaring overhead. A plain wooden table invited us to eat and play games, to chat and drink tea into the cool evening. Two bedrooms, one with bunks and soft quilts, provided us with a much-needed rest under the starry sky after a long work week. The air around it is filled with sweet memories of laughter ringing from birthday parties, an afternoon swim, and the tantalizing smells of an evening BBQ with family and friends alike.

Whenever I had a minute alone, I took some time to browse through the camp logbooks. Over forty years of memories are recorded by the varying signatures of guests. What initially was a camp is now a cottage with upgrades to meet the needs of the most modern of visitors. I thought of my parents, who would take time away and relax. I saw our family's entries noted in on the thin gray lines. Dates and kind notes from our stays recording details of treasured memories.

As a teenager, my dad and I worked to build this camp along with my brother and brother-in-law. Next to him, I swung hammers, held up braces and walls, and watched the transformation take shape before our eyes. Within a span of years but only a blink of an eye, I brought my own son and daughters out for rest and play. And now, this summer, my ten-year-old grandson fishes with me in my dad's boat at the pond.

One highlight from a random midsummer week was when Greg joined us all for an afternoon at the beach. He spent the day with his parents and sisters and their children. The time was bittersweet as he had not seen one of his sisters for two years and the other one for six. So long, too long. He had never met his youngest sister's husband or their two daughters. He had not even been to our house during that same space of time. This desperately fragile moment was a beautiful tiny step of healing. We had a picture taken of the five of us, dad, mom, brother, sister and little sister. A kodak-picture moment that whispered of hope. I am sure we all had a mixture of unique feelings that afternoon, but we all felt joy and peace as well. Thank God for all the ways He is moving in this story.

Our son has lost a lot over the past several years, huge things that may or may not ever be restored. But he knows he has the love, care, and support of his family. He has a safe place to live in a special care home. It is where he needs to be at this time in his life.

✣

Old Yellow Guitar Pick

It's just an old
yellow guitar pick
not worth much of anything
but to me
it's priceless
It has been laying neglected,
forgotten
and quietly alone
on a dresser in a spare room
I've looked at it many times
over the past few years
then walked away from it
Today I picked it up
and laid it
gently
carefully
in a drawer in my jewelry box
You wouldn't think a small
yellow guitar pick
could evoke
so many emotions
like grief
longing
aching
fear
and a tiny bit of hope

mixed in there too
Strong
talented
musical fingers
used to hold it
and with it strum
and the musician would sing songs
funny ones
sad ones
silly ones
Bob Dylan classics
and Christmas songs
even a hymn
never missing a beat
or a word
But all is quiet now
no songs
or harmonies
no strumming
or laughter
no foot tapping
along to
a favorite melody
A few tears trickle
and my heart hurts
for a while
and I whisper
a breath-prayer
that one day
One Day
that old forgotten

yellow guitar pick
will be picked up
until then
I remember…
I wait
I pray
and hope

⚜

This summer has spoken love, joy and hope to me in many ways. The song of the crickets can now be heard in mid-August, the days are getting shorter, and cool crisp mornings evolve into warm afternoons as September readies herself to say hello.

"From the rising of the sun to the place where it sets, the name of the Lord is to be praised."

—Psalms 113:3

Chapter 15

Twenty Years

"Time is what we want most, but what we use worst."

—William Penn

"In just a blink, twenty years go by faster than you think."

—Alex Daggett

This year marks twenty years of watching our son exist in a self-imposed purgatory. In September of 2025, he will be 39. It almost feels unreal that it could be that long.

The process of writing all this down the past several months has been healing for me. It has been both good to finally release these emotions, but difficult at being so raw and vulnerable. Some days, I would have to walk away and give my heart and mind a break from the darkness. Yet, writing forced me to dig deep into my soul to find the joyful moments that tell a large piece of my story too.

My son is still alive when he probably shouldn't be, and I am thankful for that each day! By the grace and kindness of God, he is. I am sure there are even a few miracles in the pages of his story, and I would be the first to listen should he ever share it. I often wonder, why does one person live through a terrible situation and another doesn't. So many big questions that are left a mystery here on earth, but I walk on in my faith, believing in God's will prevails.

With the passing of my dad and reflecting on this journey on which you have joined me, dear reader, I am led to a place of introspection. A friend of mine shared on Facebook a few weeks ago with Japanese writer Haruki Murakami:

> "And once the storm is over you won't remember how you made it through, how you managed to survive. You won't even be sure, in fact, whether the storm is really over. But one thing is certain when you come out of the storm you won't be the same person who walked in."[11]

I am not the same man I used to be. By God's grace, I am still here and pressing on. That quote really resonated with me. There are days and moments and wild storms with winds so ravaging that I can't remember how I made it through. Days when I wonder if the storm really is over or if I am in its eye.

[11] Murakami, H. (2006). *Kafka on the shore*. Vintage.

I have endured many trials and tempests, but the raging seas and bitter winds of helplessly watching my son's struggle has been the wildest for me. I was thrust into the maelstrom, rode the waves, and endured the gales all while hanging onto the Anchor, Jesus.

The anchor is a precious metaphor, reminding me of my island home and the fishing vessels that relied on the weight of the metal for stability. So many songs and hymns include the words "anchor" and "storm," including two of my favorites, "We Have an Anchor" and "A Shelter in the Time of Storm." They speak to me so much that I have even sung them myself. Jesus, my anchor, has kept me in place, in His arms, through every storm in my life.

Beyond a shadow of a doubt, the Anchor has kept my son safe and alive. I pray that it will continue to secure him the same way it has me. Prayer is a powerful weapon. I admit that I need to use it more often.

A thousand questions run through my mind about what the next twenty years will look like. I have so many prayers, hopes and concerns for my son, children, and grandchildren. Will my son be in a better spot mentally, emotionally and spiritually? Will he be living somewhere else? Will he and his children find healing and restoration? Will he and his sisters rebuild their relationship? Will my wife and I be able to help him if he wants to start a new chapter in his life? In the middle of these questions, I must trust God for each new day and surrender everything into His more than capable, loving hands.

I just turned fifty-eight. Despite a twenty-year gap between us, I feel as though I was his age just yesterday. The last twenty years have been so challenging yet rewarding. Years marked by a thousand colorful stories of joy and sadness, laughter and tears, fun and crisis, and heartache, all mixed in with faith, love and hope. Yes, hope! A love story. Our love story.

"In their hearts humans plan their course, but the Lord establishes their steps."

—Proverbs 16:9

Chapter 16
The Story Continues

*"Each life is made up of mistakes and learning, waiting and growing,
practicing patience and being persistent."*

—Rev. Billy Graham

"Every life is a story and matters to God."

—Alex Daggett

What should I label this story of mine? I am not sure. A memoir of a man who wants to share his story to help others and perhaps encourage a few readers. I am not an expert on things I have written about, but I am an experienced sojourner willing to be vulnerable to lend a hand to someone else who may be traveling on the same or similar road.

I want my story to encourage you, dear reader. Sometimes sharing one's story through vulnerability helps another person feel less alone and gives them courage. Maybe they will keep pressing on or seek help, even in the darkness. Engaging with shared stories encourages me in the same way. Maybe I am the voice you need that reminds you that you can get through whatever obstacles that roll onto your path. One step at a time.

A week ago, I sent an encouraging message to a struggling friend. We texted back and forth. The open, judgement-free reception of his feelings and concerns not only gave him a safe space to feel hidden emotions, I also could hear my own pain reflected through his words. I resonated with what he shared. In this exchange we knew we were both truly heard and understood. It was a powerful and important connection that bonded us over a small screen though miles apart. We were reminded of the fact that we are not alone, and we are being prayed for.

Unfortunately, countless families are devastated by addiction and crisis, often with minimal resources to turn to. Our family's experience taught us this firsthand. We struggled to find adequate help, but eventually, we were fortunate enough to receive the necessary support. For that, we are incredibly grateful.

My journey to trusting God and embracing my story has been long and burdensome. While I occasionally wish for a life with fewer trials, I'm aware that many more face far greater hardships. It's a harsh truth that life doesn't always offer a happy ending option, and prayers can remain unanswered or yield unexpected outcomes. So, to the parent who is on the edge of giving up, to the grieving one, to the addict who is at rock bottom, to the sibling that is holding onto hate and hope, I pray for you. You are not alone. I see you in my son's drug-battered face, in my wife's desperate tears, in my abandoned hopes. That is where those that need us most reside—in the darkest corners and the silent halls of solitary despair.

My son's story continues. We all continue day after day, walking, stumbling, believing even while doubting. It is a journey of faith. My wife wrote a beautiful poem at the end of her book, and I want to include it for you. I love the words, the message. It's our story. A love story. And God's story.

✦

Cobblestone Drive

Once upon a time 3 children lived on a Cobblestone drive

with their parents (and Kitty).

It wasn't that long ago, but it seems like it was so long ago

it could be a fairy tale, you know?

Life was easy, sunny, uncomplicated.

Weekdays meant school and activities, Friday night was pizza night

and usually a noisy sleepover.

Sunday was church and chicken dinner in a roaster - then board games

and 4-wheeler rides.

Jesus lived with us too - in the beauty and chaos of family living.

Ahhhh - I remember.

An older brother with two sisters - one a brown eyed mermaid

and the other a green-eyed busy bee.

Mostly, they lived in harmony (but not ALWAYS)

Guitars strummed, girls giggled, skateboards clacked

and Newsboys played on a CD player.

Pizza was eaten, lemonade sold, and Kraft Dinner was consumed by hungry friends.

Ball hockey scored on nets in the basement

and Polly pockets played silly in the kitchen.

Days raced by

and moments melted into years.

Slow, but fleeting - ordinary yet magical days.

The mom and dad wondered if the days would ever end

and then they did.

They stood proud as graduation caps were pinned on

and as the children tested their wings to fly.

They flew.

One girl flew on a love song to the prairies - light and pretty.

Another girl captured beautiful memories

and turned them into exquisite photo mosaics.

Two beautiful twirling tornadoes of light.

One boy, he studied and planted,

and got lost in a world he was trying to find.

Trying so hard, but losing.

Twirling in a lost world.

The mom and dad sit in an empty nest, and remember.

Reflect on the days lived a few decades ago.

Smiles, tears, laughter, prayers- all mixed together

in a swirly concoction of memories.

Three things remain: faith, hope, love

and the greatest of these is LOVE.

All are held together by a loving Father - father of them all -

the ones called mom, dad,

son, sister and little sister.

And it's not a fairy tale - it's a Love Story, written in grace

blood and redemption.

By His amazing mercy and kindness,

He is still writing their stories.

⚜

Best of days with Holly, Marissa and Greg

In Conclusion

There are no perfect parents, but there are no perfect people either. Parenting definitely isn't for the faint of heart. In this fast-paced, debit, cashless, tap-and-go world parents are faced with so many new challenges and a society which for the most part has lost its way.

I hope and pray that my story, my son's story, and my family's story will be an encouragement to someone today. If you are a struggling, and/or suffering with any of these issues I have shared, please seek help. There are many books, resources, counselors and people who truly care and want to be there for you. Don't endure the crisis on your own. Look for help and go with God, for this is how I fight my battle.

If you would like Alex and/or his wife, Joanne, to come and speak to your church, men's group, women's group, marriage session, etc., about topics discussed in this book, please contact:

Alex Daggett on Facebook or through email at alexcdaggett@gmail.com.

Acknowledgements

Thanks to Dad and Mom for being the greatest example of a faithful and loving marriage for 65 years.

Thanks to all of you who graciously proofread my book. Also thanks for your encouragement, endorsements and Pastor Brent for the foreword.

Thanks to Joppa House Publishing and Anna Rhea for your hours of editing, great ideas, suggestions, front cover design and more. You put so much into your craft.

Thanks to my three children and seven grandchildren who bring light, fun, joy and laughter into my life.

Special thanks to my beautiful wife who had the tedious task of taking my handwritten scribbled words and typing it all out for me. Man hours you sat quietly as I wrote, thought and wrote some more. Then you became my first editor, as well as typist, making my words readable.

Thanks to the good Lord, my Saviour and friend, who has seen me at my best and also at my worst. Your grace amazes me more every day.